TRADE SHOW SURVIVAL GUIDE

by Matt Hill

ARMADILLO PRESS
Mountain View, CA
press work with prestige

ISBN 0-9643633-0-5

Copyright © 1996, 1999

The **Hill** Group

1340 S. De Anza Blvd., Suite 207

San Jose, California 95129

Toll free: 888-257-7828

(408) 257-7828

(408) 257-1145 fax

email: mhill@hillgroup.com

www.hillgroup.com

If this handbook isn't fun to read, return it and we'll laugh real hard at your request for a refund.

Most training manuals offer at least *some* useful information, but it's usually presented in a dry and boring style…sort of like a staff meeting. Most people want information presented in an engaging, entertaining way. So I've re-written all of my material to try to make it fun to read.

Here's what's covered in this handbook:

- Today's Trade Show Environment
- Setting Sales and Marketing Objectives
- The Trade Show Selling Process
- Presentations and Demonstrations
- Group Dynamics
- Crowd Control
- The Basics: DOs and DON'Ts of Professional Behavior

Here's what's not covered in this handbook:

▶ How to Discourage Sales Managers From Wearing Plaid Pants.

▶ How to Lower Caffeine Levels In Trade Show Managers.

▶ Proper Use Of A Whoopee Cushion On The Show Floor.

▶ The Rationale Behind The "Circle of Executives" Bonding Ritual.

▶ Seven Tips On How To Jettison Your Pocket Protector Before Cruising The Show.

Table of Contents

TRADE SHOW ENVIRONMENT

Why go? Who cares?

It used to be that companies exhibited at trade shows because they thought they had to. If they weren't there, they felt people would think they were out of the business.

Today, companies exhibit at trade shows because they think they have to. If they're not there, they now feel people would think they were out of the business. So a lot has changed.

What has also **not** changed is management's insistence on accountability and ROI from trade shows. The nerve! Why don't they feel that way about their "fact finding" trips to the Cayman Islands? Anyway, if your company decides trade shows are worth it, and **statistics prove that they are,*** why not be as productive as possible?

Can you say "Competitive Advantage"?

There is a unique environment at trade shows. You have the opportunity to wait 20 minutes for a $16 hot dog and coke lunch. You get to wait 15 minutes to use a phone only to find out you're missing an important customer meeting.

*I know I read it somewhere.

But trade shows are also the only place I know of where you can go through two or three steps of the sales cycle in under 10 minutes. For an outside sales person, to go through two or three steps of the sales cycle by making appointments and going to meetings, can take weeks. Even longer if they have to play golf.

You can realize a significant advantage over your competitors if you know how to effectively work at trade shows. **I challenge you to take a new look at what you do at trade shows, how you do it, and try some new skills and techniques.**

There are over 10,000 trade shows in the U.S. every year. Over six billion dollars are spent supporting them. So if you and your company decide to keep doing the same old thing in the same old way, I've got plenty of other prospects. I don't need you.

Enough pleasantries. Take a shot at the "Trade Show Puzzle" on the next page to see how you stack up against the typical exhibit staff working trade shows today.

TRADE SHOW CROSSWORD PUZZLE

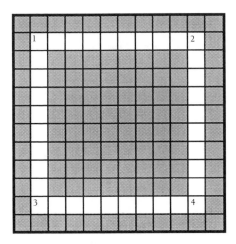

Clues

Across

1. Where you can take prospects through 2 or 3 steps of the sales cycle in only 6 minutes.

2. The antitheses of the primordial theory of self-determination relative to Faustian and Jungian head cleaning (hint: you idiot, there is no "2 across").

3. Where you have a golden opportunity to blow it with both your customers and your boss at the same time.

Down

1. Where many leads are generated but rarely followed-up.

2. Where work is hard, hours are long, food is lousy . . . no, it's not home.

3. Your Boss' IQ, expressed in base 7.

> *1-3 correct: You're an idiot*
> *4 correct: There's hope*
> *5-6 correct: Too much prozac*

This page
intentionally
left blank
because
what I had
originally planned
to write here
had way too many big words
for you
to sound out.

KEY POINTS

Trade Show Environment

Take trade shows seriously.

You can have more meaningful face-to-face interactions per hour, than anywhere else.

You'll gain a competitive advantage.

Trade shows generate revenue.

Qualified leads result in sales.

You can go through two or three steps of the sales cycle efficiently and do it every six minutes.

There is a separate skill set.

You need a combination of outside and retail selling expertise *plus* the ability to function productively in a "show business" setting.

SETTING REASONABLE OBJECTIVES

Besides free food, why go to pre-show meetings?

So here you are at the mandatory pre-show meeting. The trade show manager is again telling everyone not to puke in the booth, no wine coolers, etc. Thank god there's coffee.

Then comes the discussion on "why we're going to the show." Your wonderful marketing department is really on the ball this time. They've come up with the following objectives:

(1) To announce our "new" product …for the third time

(2) To demonstrate our commitment to the open systems environment through oral hygiene and regular professional care

(3) To communicate our support to our distributors and VARs

(4) To boldly go where no one has gone before, and

(5) To party

SMART Objectives, DUMB ideas

The problem with most objectives is you can't tell what to do to meet them…you can't get your arms around them …it's like trying to hug Rush Limbaugh. To really succeed, you should hire me to help you come up with your objectives. I would have them be:

SPECIFIC
MEASURABLE
ACHIEVABLE
RELEVANT
TIME DEPENDENT

Notice how the first letters of the words spell SMART? This is called an acronym; "acro" from the Latin "acronous" meaning "collector of the wizard's drool," and "nym" from the Russian "nyet-nym-nyet" meaning "not now, I've got a headache." Simple.

If your show's objectives don't meet these five SMART criteria, everyone working in the booth will have a different idea of what they need to do to meet them. For example; suppose one of your objectives is to "collect leads." For Bob, that means standing outside the convention center asking passersby if they have any spare leads. For Debbie, it means paying $5 for any visitor, qualified or not, to fill out a lead form.

But, if everyone's on the same dance card, singing from the same hymn book, paddling the same canoe, drinking from the same glass, eating the same taco, putting on the same pair of pants…well, anyway, your staff will be more professional and feel more like a team.

Trade Show Objectives

Every booth has less visitors sometimes and gets really congested other times. When there are only staff in the booth, talk with any visitor, for any length of time. But when other, and possibly more qualified, visitors show up, it's time to be efficient by using the skills and techniques offered on the following pages.

Prioritize the following types of visitors according to whom you would talk to first.

PRIORITY	TYPE OF VISITOR
_____	One of your own colleagues
_____	Booth beggar
_____	Competitor
_____	Qualified visitor
_____	Current customer
_____	Another exhibitor
_____	Attractive visitor
_____	Former employee
_____	Business associate
_____	Your boss
_____	Your boss' boss
_____	Your bookie
_____	Your parole officer
_____	Your psychiatrist
_____	Old drinking buddy
_____	Your mom

Trade Show Objectives Quiz

1. *Marketing's trade show objectives (circle all that apply)*
   a. Introduce new products.
   b. Communicate a corporate message or image.
   c. Collect leads.
   d. Wear the new suit.
   e. Schmooze with executives.

2. *Sales' trade show objectives (make a square around all that apply)*
   a. Write orders.
   b. Meet prospects and customers.
   c. Collect leads.
   d. Strategize with colleagues (translation: stand in a circle, ignore visitors, decide where to have dinner).
   e. Dutifully "support" the clowns in marketing and their stupid trade shows.

3. *Your personal objectives (make a trapezoid around all that apply)*
   a. Get through the day even though you're tried and/or hung over
   b. Hope your only two customers show up so you won't get in trouble with your manager
   c. Make it through the show without anyone finding out you have no idea what your products look like, how they work, or how much they cost.
   d. Look for a better job

KEY POINTS

Objectives

 Focus on the show's objectives.

Treat trade shows as a serious sales and marketing effort.

Make it business first.

But you can still have fun.

© The Hill Group • (408) 257-7828

MANAGING YOUR OWN EXPECTATIONS

Can every visitor be brought to the point of wanting to purchase your products/services? How about some visitors? How about one visitor? Probably not. Anyway, most visitors are going to see right through your Multi-Level Marketing scheme.

Have modest, achievable objectives for each visitor. Don't try to do too much. You'll wind up wasting your time. By using your outstanding ability (just kidding!) to ask questions, you will be able to find out where a visitor is in your sales cycle. Visitors could be at any of the steps in your sales cycle.

Step 1	Step 2	Step 3	Step 4	Step 5

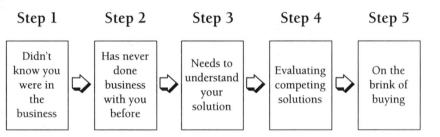

| Didn't know you were in the business | Has never done business with you before | Needs to understand your solution | Evaluating competing solutions | On the brink of buying |

What can you do to move a qualified visitor from one step to the next? Offer a bribe? No, not a good idea, leave the bribe taking to purchasing. Find out where they are in your sales cycle and then offer a solution delivered via conversation, presentation, demonstration, or by threatening them with physical harm.

Should you consider yourself successful if you can move visitors just one or two steps along in your sales cycle? Absolutely. It could take you an hour or more to move that one more additional step. Don't do it. Get a commitment for a follow-up call and do it then.

Should you change what you talk about depending upon the visitor's level of expertise? No, you idiot, act like a robot (or product manager—same thing) and say the same exact thing to everybody. Talking about arcane computer code to a decision maker type who's looking for a business solution is really stupid. Tailor what you say to make a fit with the varying levels of expertise and interests the different visitors have. You should have a customized objective for each visitor.

**WRONG WAY
You Idiot!**

RIGHT WAY
You got the sale!

Sales Cycle Exercise

Put the steps below in their proper sequence (for a hint, we're giving you step #1.)

STEP #	SALES CYCLE ACTIVITY
	On knees begging for order
	Never heard of you or your company
	You're competing for the business
	Bringing in Sales Manager to save order
	Bringing in VP of Sales to save order
	Bringing in President to save order
	Bringing in a large hand gun to save order
	Heard of your company, but not a customer
1	Just got another great lead from a trade show
	P.O. is being generated in Budapest
	Order on hold, purchasing manager in Maui on vacation
	Follow-up appointment to present proposal
	Printer out of paper, proposal on hold 'til paper goes on sale
	Make presentation to customer—take whoopee cushion
	Ask customer about needs and problems
	Handle "Mind your own business!" objection
	Initial sales call, wear clean shirt, use deodorant
	Got the order, that's one in a row
	Customer coming to showroom for demo, remove camels
	Equipment fails, customer leaves showroom
	Frustrated, you kick failed equipment
	You go to urgent care for broken toe

Writer's Block—Blank Page

KEY POINTS

Managing Your Own Expectations

➤ *Have modest expectations.*
   Realize not every visitor will be a customer.

   A reasonable objective is moving qualified
   visitors just 1 or 2 steps through the sales cycle.

➤ *Understand your sales cycle.*
   There are probably 5 or 6 discreet steps.

   Ask questions to find out where the visitor is
   in your sales cycle.

➤ *Determine their level of knowledge.*
   Find out how much the visitor knows about
   your products, services, technology, market, etc.

➤ *Customize an objective for each visitor.*

© The Hill Group • (408) 257-7828

MANAGING VISITORS' EXPECTATIONS
They shouldn't expect too much working with you

It's true! Visitors attending trade shows actually pay money to wander around and get harassed by low-life, smelly exhibit staff people (that's you). Why do they do this? Why do they put up with $8 bone dry turkey sandwiches and annoying, overly cheerful, and ultimately useless exhibit staff personnel (that's you again). Because it's a break from the monotony of their own offices, dealing with same trivial issues, working with the same boring people. The question is, "How can you get the key points out of this book without having to wade through this juvenile humor?" Wait a minute, that's not the question. The real question is, "What do visitors expect to happen when they come into my booth?" Here are four generic visitor expectations and the reasons why they need to managed:

1. Visitors expect that you're there to answer as many questions as they can ask.

Yes, part of your job is to answer visitor's questions. But if you spend a lot of time answering a visitor's questions before you find out if they deserve more and more of your time, especially when your booth is busy, you run the risk of wasting your time with an unqualified visitor.

2. Visitors think that even if they have to queue up and wait for you, they'll get a one-on-one conversation.

One-on-one conversations are great, just ask your spouse. Wait, bad example. But if it's busy in the booth and visitors are waiting to talk to you, they might get tired of waiting and walk away. And they could have been your hottest prospect at the show! Add waiting visitors to your conversations, or at least acknowledge them, so they don't leave your booth without some contact.

3. Visitors expect every one of their questions to be answered completely and to their satisfaction.

Sometimes you can't, or shouldn't, answer every question. Should you comment on your CEO's constant string of sexual harassment lawsuits? Should you comment on your new product's 30 minute AMTBF (Average Mean Time Between Failure)? And what about that technical question you do know the answer to but will take 45 minutes to answer? Some questions should be deflected, neglected, and selected to handle later.

4. Visitors assume they'll be able to walk away with whatever free thing you're giving away.

Get ready for the Booth Beggars! Once your free hat, T-shirt, Frisbee, or whatever you're giving away is seen on the show floor, visitors will start asking you how they can get one. If there's a qualifier, like seeing your theater presentation or visiting a demo station, tell them. If they have a problem, let the booth manager handle it, don't waste your semi-valuable time arguing. Also, be honest about your own abilities; your customer service skills probably suck.

5. Visitors assume they're going to be able to buy their lunch at a trade show for under $22.50.

Visitor's Perspective Quiz

Which drawing below best represents what visitors think?

1

2

3

4

5

6

7

8

This has just been one big ruse because I just happen to like optical illusions.

KEY POINTS

Managing Visitor Expectations

➤ *Most visitors assume the following:*

They'll have a one-on-one conversation with you for as long as they have questions to ask.

All of their questions will be answered.

They will receive whatever you're giving away.

➤ *Control the conversation.*

Manage the topic and time by asking questions and controlling the conversation.

➤ *Don't let visitors wait.*

Add them to on-going conversations.

➤ *Defer unanswerable questions.*

Commit to returning an answer after the show.

➤ *Don't waste time managing give-aways.*

© The Hill Group • (408) 257-7828

THE TRADE SHOW SELLING PROCESS

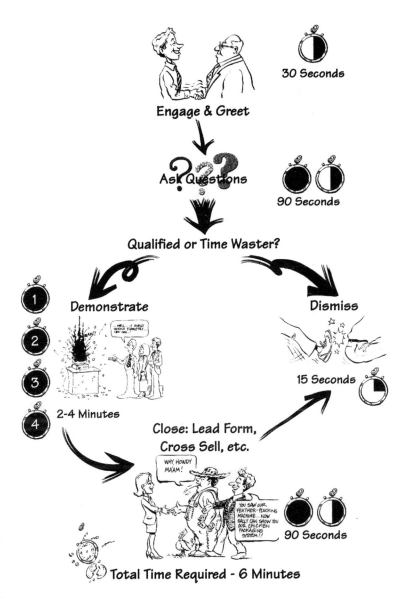

Okay, for you visual types here's a flowchart giving you a graphical representation of the **Trade Show Selling Process**. With your finger, press on the step in the process to see how stupid you can look because nothing will happen.

TRADE SHOW SELLING PROCESS WORD SEARCH

Find the words in the list below. Look for them vertically, horizontally, and backwards.

```
P  P  T  O  D  I  N  A  E  R  U  O  Y  P  E  E
A  H  K  R  E  J  S  I  S  S  O  B  G  R  A  M
R  U  H  G  I  N  S  O  L  C  O  L  N  E  T  I
E  E  S  O  N  N  D  B  O  O  Z  E  I  S  I  T
V  D  I  S  M  I  S  S  I  N  G  S  T  E  T  F
O  P  R  I  P  E  Y  D  U  M  B  E  E  N  I  O
G  U  D  U  C  K  E  F  F  S  A  T  E  T  A  E
N  T  T  X  N  A  P  E  I  L  D  T  R  A  W  T
A  S  B  O  S  K  P  E  U  L  A  E  G  T  T  S
H  O  G  G  N  I  T  E  K  R  A  M  M  I  N  A
L  O  D  N  A  S  D  N  U  O  P  U  Q  O  A  W
T  E  R  M  I  N  A  T  I  O  N  U  Q  N  C  W
```

Word List

Greeting	Qualifying	Dismissing
Presentation	Demo	Closing
Drunk	Hangover	Termination
Stupid	Marketing	Ideas
Cantwait	Togo	Home

KEY POINTS

The Trade Show Selling Process
Total Time Required—6 minutes

Engage and Greet—30 seconds
Take control by asking open-ended questions.

Question and Qualify—90 seconds
Ask questions specific to their situation.
Ask questions specific to your solutions.
Ask qualifying questions.

Dismiss—10 seconds
Shake hands and thank them for stopping by.

Demonstrate—2-4 minutes
Show what excites them, not you.

Close—90 seconds
Fill out a lead form, cross-sell, dismiss them.

ENGAGE

Non-violent ways of getting attention

Sure, it may be more fun to yank a show visitor out of the aisle by their bolo tie, or it might be challenging to surround, capture, and carry a visitor into your booth; but your beautifully designed and perfectly located booth should be *the* primary tool for attracting visitors.

Now realize that the perfect trade show for most visitors would have *no one in the booths at all*—just brochures piled on the counters. In other words, most visitors …just like your family…are trying to avoid you. Aside from your incurable halitosis, don't give them any reason *not* to come into your booth.

Here are a few things that work…most of the time… to attract visitors:

1. Make eye contact. Look them in the eye first, then, if you need to, look at their badge. Don't stare, just make friendly, interested eye contact.

2. Have open body language. This doesn't mean an open shirt, blouse, or fly. It means standing comfortably, with a pleasant look on your face (you'll probably have to fake the "pleasant look" part).

3. Act interested in your products and services (extensive acting may be required). When there is nothing to do in the booth, act interested in what is on display. Play with it a little…but not with your back to the aisle…and be ready to engage any visitor that happens by.

Try the sorting exercise on the following page to test your knowledge of what attracts or repulses visitors.

ENGAGING EXERCISE

Put an "X" in the "Attracts" or "Repulses" column to describe each Action, Appearance, or Behavior

ACTION, APPEARANCE, OR BEHAVIOR	ATTRACTS	REPULSES
1. Looking like the classic trade show geek: just-won-the-lottery smile, fresh scrubbed look, etc.		
2. Standing in a circle talking among yourselves.		
3. Eating, drinking, reading.		
4. Communicating real openness; arms crossed, scowl on face.		
5. Quietly humming the words to "Feelings."		
6. Using computer, back to aisle.		
7. Tossing popcorn into the air and trying to catch it in your mouth.		
8. Having a glazed look; you're somewhere else...on a beach in Hawaii, mai tai in hand,...		
9. Watching an actor play Babe Ruth in the next booth.		

Surprised with the answers?

KEY POINTS

Engage

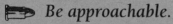 *Be approachable.*

    Smile.

    Make eye contact.

    Have open body language.

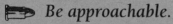 *Stand away from colleagues.*

    Don't give visitors any reason not to make contact with you.

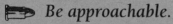 *Be a good listener.*

    Don't interrupt.

    Ask follow-up questions.

    Pay attention to the visitor's answers.

GREET
Personal stretch time: being pleasant

"Get in here and buy something you low-life grunt!" is an opening that used to work at trade shows. Think about it...in one short sentence there was a greeting, call to action, and closing. But times have changed. Now, this tactic is only effective when it's the end of the quarter and you're only 35% of plan.

Greetings are tough because you have to take a risk and it can be a little scary. If only we could reach inside ourselves and yank out those fears. If only we could reconcile our ancient childhood traumas that continue to affect us. If only our self-esteem were high enough so we didn't have to disguise our voice at the McDonald's drive thru. If only I could charge you for therapy too.

Get your crayon ready

The only way you can have an effective greeting that is comfortable to say is to design it yourself. Here are some opening lines; adapt them to your own style:

1. Tell me, what do you know about our company?
2. What products/services are you interested in?
3. Tell me what kinds of needs/applications you have.
4. What interests you in this section of our booth?
5. How are you enjoying the show, mooseface?

Notice that each open-ended question begins with "Tell me" "What" or "How." Words like these usually solicit a longer answer than "yes" or "no" or "get lost." The greeting is your only real opportunity to establish rapport with a visitor. You don't usually have time to discuss your impending surgery or recent arrest. And remember, rapport is, or isn't, established within the first minute.

Maintaining control without Depends®

One more point about the greeting before you do the cute little quiz on the next page. It is very important to take control of the conversation by asking the *first* question.

When *you* have control of the conversation, you can qualify, dismiss, and/or get a lead form filled out quickly. If the visitor is asking the questions, you could be stuck with an unqualified, spittle-spewing visitor, who ends up wasting your time.

If the visitor asks the first question, respond with "The Reverse;" answer their question with a question. The Reverse works like this; after they ask their question say, "That's a good question, but let me ask you a question," or "Before I answer your question, tell me how you've managed to…escape prosecution for so long?" The reverse puts you back in control of the conversation. Try it out on a traffic cop.

Greeting Fill-in Quiz

1. To control the conversation so I can meet the show's objectives, I need to ask the _____ question.

2. If the visitor asks the first question, I should use The _____ technique to regain control of the conversation.

3. The _____ should do most of the talking.

4. After I've qualified two or three visitors, the best place in the booth for a nap is _____.

Answers: Alexander Hamilton, Cream of Tartar, Iron Butterfly, You get down off a duck.

Use the "Elevator Answer"

Here are two typical requests from visitors: "Wow, your booth looks totally cluttered! Tell me about everything!" or "This new product of yours probably sucks like the rest of the junk you produce, but tell me all about it anyway." How would you handle them? I don't think they're opportunities for you to launch into 20 minute answers for either of them. Use the Elevator Answer. It takes 30 seconds, gives a complete answer, then you can get back to asking your questions. It's as if you're actually in an elevator and you have limited time to talk about your company or your products.

Here are the elements of the Elevator Answer: tortilla, beans, rice, guacamole, lettuce, tomato, salsa…no wait, those are the elements for a burrito. I'm always getting them mixed up. Here we go: (1) say something irrefutable; our company does this or this new product does this, (2) give a credibility piece; we've been doing this for 15 years or some of our clients include the top companies in our industry, (3) talk about two or three generic benefits most people who know your industry can relate to, and (4) finish with a call-to-action; you ought to come by our booth (if you're actually in an elevator) or I think we should start out by showing you this product.

Ah, an almost
totally blank page:
nothing to absorb;
nothing to think about;
probably reminds you
of your last one-on-one
with your manager.

Key Points

Greet

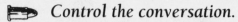 *Control the conversation.*

> Ask the first question.
>
> Use the reverse...answering a question with a question...to regain control.
>
> Use questions to direct the conversation.

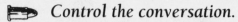 *Ask "open ended" questions.*

> Open ended questions cannot be answered by "yes" or "no."
>
> Open ended questions will give you information.

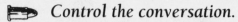 *Build rapport in two minutes.*

> Again, be a good listener.
>
> Focus on *their* areas of interest.

© The Hill Group • (408) 257-7828

ASK QUESTIONS

2 ears, 1 mouth, 0 or Ø brain

This is the first step toward one of our major goals of working in the booth: spending time with qualified visitors and dismissing visitors who waste your time. And, yes, these techniques also work on your own company's executive and management types.

By asking questions that are relative to your company's products and services...that's assuming you know what your products and services are...you can begin to weed out the tire-kickers from real prospects. Questions that help uncover needs usually begin on a more global or general scale and then move to more specific areas in need of improvement, upgrade, or solutions.

Shut up and listen

Now I know this next concept goes against your natural tendencies, but here goes. Try to focus the conversation, by asking questions, on what the *visitor* is interested in, *not* what interests you. You may be totally excited about the new clock speed of your mother board, but every mother  will be bored, and fathers, sons, and daughters too if you talk about it before asking if the visitor cares about it.

This is a key concept so I'm going to say it again. Talk about *their* business, not yours. Ask what they like about your products and services, don't tell them what you like. Ask questions to uncover problems and areas of frustration, don't bore them with your guesses about what they care about. This isn't a marriage...don't treat it like one. Time for another quiz.

ASK QUESTIONS QUIZ

True, False, or...

STATEMENT	TRUE	FALSE	WHO CARES?
1. Uncovering needs is best done with a four page survey.			
2. Asking questions is only for sales-types.			
3. Asking questions is too hard, I want to go home.			
4. I shouldn't care about not caring about whether or not they don't have any needs that I don't care about.			
5. If you don't uncover a visitor's needs, they might waste your time.			
6. If you're reading this, you're wasting your time.			
7. Visitors wearing polyester are easier to talk to.			

KEY POINTS

Ask Questions

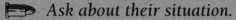 *Ask about their situation.*

  What products and services they are using.

  What challenges they are encountering.

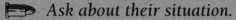 *Ask which problems they want to solve or what they want to improve.*

  Talk about how other customers have solved similar problems.

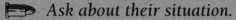 *Ask why it's important to solve the problem or improve the situation.*

  Direct the answers toward lost time, money, productivity, etc.

Qualified or Time Waster?

You're the judge and jury

Don't let anyone waste your time at trade shows. Time wasting should remain where it is...at staff meetings. You need to focus

on meeting the objectives of the show and not let any stupid visitors get in your way. I realize this is a new concept, but stay with me.

Maybe, instead of taking an hour with just any nerd to discuss the proper way of rubber-banding hair into a ponytail so that it avoids getting caught in pocket protectors, you could actually find out if this person is the CEO of a multi-zillion dollar corporation and whose VISA card is poised to purchase $500K of your product right now.

Short Subject: Attention Spans

If you have control of the conversation, you can proceed to qualify each visitor. Qualifying should only take about two minutes (a visitor's attention span). After two minutes, you should dismiss them if they're not qualified or, if they are qualified, continue to work with them for up to six minutes (your attention span).

Qualify visitors by asking qualifying questions (I know this is a tough relationship for you to comprehend). Qualifying questions usually focus on the following criteria:

    (0.5)   need for your product or service
    (1.7)   role of visitor in decision-making process
    (2.3)   buying timeframe within your sales cycle
    (3.6)   funding (budget, cash, trading cards)
    (4.0)   size of their head.

What distinguishes a "Hot" lead from just a qualified lead is when the visitor wants to be contacted by a salesperson (caution; people who want to see salespeople usually need counseling).

These and other more specific qualifiers need to be determined before the show according to the average cost and sales cycle of your products and services. Take time to design your own qualifying questions using the handy selection matrix on the next page.

DESIGNING QUALIFYING QUESTIONS

Match up any "Opening" from column #1 with any "Qualifying Factor" from column #2

OPENINGS	QUALIFYING FACTORS
Tell me,…	…what is frustrating about the way you're handling that now?
Before I show you our new product,…	…why is it important to solve this problem?
Let me ask you this question…	…is there a budget to solve this problem?
To help me focus this demo,…	…when does your company plan on making a decision?
Good question! To answer it, let me ask you a question…	…what is your decision making process?
Before we begin, let me ask you a question…	…didn't I see you on "America's Most Wanted," last week?
Gosh, I didn't know they still made green polyester leisure suits, and…	…would you mind taking our computer out from under your jacket and putting it back where you found it?
You have an interesting facial architecture,…	…when is your plastic surgery scheduled?
I don't normally talk to stupid people but…	…do you worry about Greenpeace finding you on the beach?

KEY POINTS

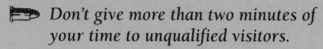

Qualify

➤ *Don't give more than two minutes of your time to unqualified visitors.*

➤ *Weave qualifying questions into your conversation.*

> Buying authority; decision maker, recommender, influencer.

> Buying time frame; 0-3 months, 3-6 months, 6+ months.

> Budget; fully funded, some budget, no budget now.

➤ *Every visitor should earn the right to a demonstration.*

© The Hill Group • (408) 257-7828

DISMISS

Disposing of Human Debris

This is one of my favorite parts. Dismissing unqualified visitors is easy to do, it works, it will absolutely make you more productive, and the visitor won't even know what happened. Sort of like when you pick-pocket key customers during a demo.

You dismiss visitors for either of two reasons. First, through your wonderful ability to ask qualifying questions, you discover that they are lacking at least one of the following:

(.5) A need for your product/service

(1) A reasonable buying time frame

(2) Funding or a budget

(3) A role in influencing, recommending, or making a buying decision (maybe they're at the show because their car had room for five).

The second reason to dismiss visitors is that they are one of the following:

(1) Anal types who want a complete education on all of your products

(2) One-person companies with the buying potential of a bag lady

(3) Students

(4)   Competitors with bad disguises

(5)   Personal friends (that's assuming you have any) or

(6)   People from your own company who don't have booth duty but drop by to waste your time (usually executives).

(7)   A totally qualified visitor whose time with you is finished

Dump Visitors Delicately

Use the "Letterman Dismissal" to dismiss someone. This is named after David Letterman, the late night talk show host. When he's finished interviewing someone, he looks them in the eye, sticks out his hand, says something like, "It was great to talk with you. Thanks for coming by.," shakes the guest's hand, and they're dismissed.

So, to dismiss unqualified visitors; make eye contact, shake their hand and say, "Thanks for stopping by. Have a great show!"

That's it . . . they're dismissed! They're done. It's over. They'll walk away. It really works. Try it on your boss, spouse, kids, Jehovahs Witnesses, insurance salespeople, etc.

DISMISSAL FLOWCHART EXERCISE

Which step is first, second,....sixth?

DISMISSAL ACTIVITY   STEP NUMBER

Make eye contact
and shake their hand.   ◯

Out of gratitude,
send Matt Hill $100.   ◯

They'll walk away,
they're dismissed!   ◯

Ask qualifying
questions.   ◯

Decide if they're
qualified.   ◯

Say, "thanks for
stopping by."   ◯ ⬅

If you haven't figured it out, you moron, put the numbers 1-6 in the circles.

© The Hill Group • (408) 257-7828

KEY POINTS

Dismissing

 Use the "Letterman" technique.

  Make eye contact.

  Shake hands.

  Thank them for stopping by.

 Dismiss visitors who are:

  Unqualified; wasting your time.

  Unqualified; will not help you meet your objectives.

  Qualified; and it's time to move on—use it to end conversations.

  Competitors.

  Anyone else you want to get rid of.

DEMONSTRATE

A Demo Memo

If the visitor is qualified, they have now earned the right for more of your time. You may need to launch into a demonstration to help you reach your objectives; getting a lead form filled out, making an appointment, sale, or closing for the next step in your sales process.

But a lot of things can happen that aren't so great when you do a demonstration;

(1) They take a lot of your semi-valuable time

(2) You can get sidetracked talking about unimportant issues—like your recent parole or

(3) You can embarrass yourself if the equipment fails, or if they smell your breath.

© The Hill Group • (408) 257-7828

Your Demos Probably Suck

Trade show demos are not necessarily different from presentations in the real world. Like in the real world, they should have an objective, focus on the prospect's interest, and have a beginning, middle, and end. I'm certain your demos are like this, so you should have no trouble putting together an effective trade show demo. The truth is, I'm lying. Your demos are probably poorly planned and delivered. Thanks . . . just a lucky guess.

Come to each show prepared with *two* demos. The first one is two minutes long, and is used to qualify visitors or to give a broad overview of your company. The clear objective of the second demo is to move this qualified visitor to the next step in your sales process. It should last no more than four (4, IV, 144/6-20) minutes. Pay attention, you techno-nerds! Talk about what the *visitor* is interested in, not what interests you. Most visitors couldn't care less about your personal insignificant contributions to your product's development.

I also recommend that you use the Adult Learning Theory: Go to a bar, get them drunk, and they'll believe anything you say. No, no, that's not it. Here it is:

   (1) Tell them what you you're going to tell them
   (2) Tell them, and then,
   (3) Tell them what you told them.

Also, tell them how long your demonstration or presentation is going to take.

To get a short break from doing demonstrations or presentations when the booth is really busy, make a more formal presentaion. Tell the audience how long you'll take and then stick to it! Finish up by saying something like, "Before I take a short break, I'll take two more questions."

DEMONSTRATION QUIZ

We've given you the answers, what are the questions?

1. The answer is: "Back to the aisle."
   What's the question?

   a. What do trade show shoplifters say to begin their escape?
   b. What do booth beggars say after getting a free pen?
   c. What you shouldn't have while doing a demo?

2. The answer is: "Two short ones."
    What's the question?

    a. How could you describe an 8 oz. beer and Danny DeVito?
    b. What did the tiny twos and tiny threes want their
        neighbors, the ones, to be so they could feel superior?
    c. Describe what kinds of demos to be prepared with for
        a show?

3. The answer is: "Down to the component level."
    What's the question?

    a. What's a common response to the elevator operator's
        destination request at *Nerds USA*?
    b. What might a romantic engineer request of his partner in
        the heat of passion?
    c. When doing a demo, what level of interest should you
        not be willing to go to as it will most likely waste
        your time?

KEY POINTS

Demonstrate

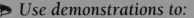 **Use demonstrations to:**

Provide a brief (< 2 min.) overview of your company and its products and services.

Further develop interest in your products.

Qualify visitors.

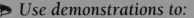 **Have two demonstrations ready.**

A short one, (< 2 min.) to qualify visitors.

A longer one (< 4 min.) focused on the visitor's application(s).

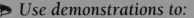 **Be in control of the demonstration.**

Have a beginning, middle, and end.

Have a clear objective for the demo; **close for something.**

Close

Closing Isn't Just for ~~Slime Bags~~ Salespeople

In the exhibit booth, there are three typical closes:

(1) filling out a lead form;

(2) escorting visitors to another area in the booth or

(3) dismissing visitors.

There is a fourth kind of close that is a little more obscure and is not recommended for the novice; begging or groveling. For tips on this technique ask to be a part of a budget meeting.

Here are the names of some common closing techniques: puppy dog, sharp angle, assumptive, Ben Franklin, alternative, power close, crash and burn, test, and limited supply.

Here are some names for people who use these closing techniques in place of good communication and selling skills: dolt, moron, idiot, air head, numbskull, tuna brain, Regional Sales Manager, idiot stick, mush brain, and credit manager.

If you don't like the word "close" because it sounds too sales-like, how about "commitment," or "call for action," or "agree on the next step," or "reaching a mutually agreed upon course of action," or "reaching a consensus to continue along a vector that will manifest itself sequentially as actionable activities toward a mutually acceptable agreement to continue to develop our relationship and, possibly, provide solutions."

Try Something Different: Be Honest

If you didn't skip, miss, or forget a step in the *Trade Show Selling Process,* closing will be easy and natural…just like shoplifting at your favorite store. Of the three possible closes listed earlier, the lead form is truly the best way to get additional information and additional service to your visitors.

Go ahead and tell them this so they can get the lead form filled out and avoid your long, boring presentation. Yes, honesty sometimes works; but I don't recommend its use on a regular basis.

Get Good At Visitor Manipulation

Fill out the lead form yourself or work together to fill it out. But be bold about asking, it's not like your complexion; something to be ashamed of. Visitors are used to filling out lead forms, it's no big deal. Just make sure all the information you want and need is asked for on the lead form. It's the only record of your conversation.

In closing, remember that closing isn't like executive recruiting; slimy or low-class. It concludes conversations, clarifies commitments and next steps, and it helps you work with as many people as possible.

TRADE SHOW SELLING GAME

See if you can make it to the finish!

Move a square each time you do something right.
You're right, this could take forever.

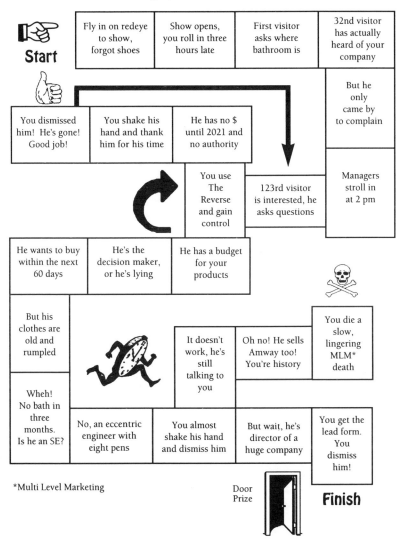

Start

| Fly in on redeye to show, forgot shoes | Show opens, you roll in three hours late | First visitor asks where bathroom is | 32nd visitor has actually heard of your company |

But he only came by to complain

| You dismissed him! He's gone! Good job! | You shake his hand and thank him for his time | He has no $ until 2021 and no authority |

| | You use The Reverse and gain control | 123rd visitor is interested, he asks questions | Managers stroll in at 2 pm |

| He wants to buy within the next 60 days | He's the decision maker, or he's lying | He has a budget for your products |

| But his clothes are old and rumpled | | It doesn't work, he's still talking to you | Oh no! He sells Amway too! You're history | You die a slow, lingering MLM* death |

| Wheh! No bath in three months. Is he an SE? | No, an eccentric engineer with eight pens | You almost shake his hand and dismiss him | But wait, he's director of a huge company | You get the lead form. You dismiss him! |

*Multi Level Marketing

Door Prize

Finish

© The Hill Group • (408) 257-7828

Hey! Quit reading this!
This page is blank
you idiot!

Key Points

Close

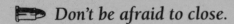 *Don't be afraid to close.*

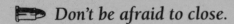 *Typical closes:*

Fill out a lead form together.

Cross-sell; escort qualified visitors to another station or area in the exhibit booth.

Hand them some product information or brochures.

Dismiss them; end the conversation.

© The Hill Group • (408) 257-7828

CROSS-SELL

Establish Your Own Escort Service

Cross-selling, not to be confused with cross-dressing (appropriate at some shows and, of course, at national sales meetings), is defined as *escorting* <u>qualified</u> visitors to other areas in the booth.

Cross-selling is *important* because:

1. I'm the expert, it's my book, and I said so.

2. You might introduce your visitors, and probably yourself, to a number of your company's products and services that neither of you were aware of.

3. It's entertaining to see how long someone will follow you aimlessly through the booth. Buy a pedometer, have a contest!

4. You can off-load any pea-brain visitor onto your least favorite colleague.

Cross-selling is *easy* because:

1. Visitors can be like sheep—and like that clown from accounting—they'll follow you anywhere. All you have to do is start walking toward another part of the booth (Attention engineers: do not attempt any walking while chewing gum).

2. Most visitors want to know what's in the rest of your exhibit booth. You'll be doing them a service by offering to show them around. You'll be doing me a service by buying 50 more copies of this handbook.

CROSS-SELLING WORD JUMBLE

Unscramble the highlighted words below to learn more about Cross Selling

1. To find out if a visitor might want to visit other areas in your exhibit booth, **kas**!

2. Don't just tell about or point visitors to other areas in your booth, **rsetoc** them.

3. Cross selling is easy to do. Just keep talking and start **iwklagn.** They'll follow.

4. When you introduce visitors to another member of your exhibit staff, it's called a **dnah-fof.**

5. Cross-selling is important because it can generate incremental revenue and keep your company from laying off **ddea oodw** like you.

6. In baseball, the four ways of safely reaching first base without hitting the ball are a **kalw, ith tterab, popddre rhtdi kersti,** and **hcaretc eeeeicfrtn.**

7. If you try to cross sell cross-eyed cross-dressers from across the room, they might become **ssorc.**

8. If one of your executives has just concluded an "executive tour" of the booth for some important clients and the only thing the clients wanted to talk about was "the expanding Kleenex marketplace," maybe they're subtly hinting that your executives should do a pre-tour **oorgab** check.

Answers: 1. Ask, 2. escort, 3. walking, 4. hand-off, 5. dead wood, 6. walk, hit batter, dropped third strike, catcher interference.

Unscramble the words below.

anbkl aepg

KEY POINTS

Cross-Sell

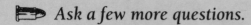 *Ask a few more questions.*

To find out if some of your other products and services are of interest.

To find out if they should visit another area or station in the exhibit booth.

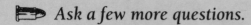 *Escort them around the booth.*

Don't just point or direct them.

Make a personal introduction.

© The Hill Group • (408) 257-7828

OFFENDING INTERNATIONAL VISITORS

So They Talk Funny, Be Sensitive
Their money buys stuff too!

Hey! Look at that…is he wearing a dress? Wow take a look at that funny little round hat! Why doesn't he talk more better English!

What's wrong with these visitors? Nothing. These are international visitors and they deserve the same respect you show your ~~parole officer~~ domestic customers. Because it costs foreign companies a ton of money to send their people to U.S. shows, they usually send higher level people who have high levels of responsibility and authority. You're going to miss the boat if you're not sensitive to other countries' business and interpersonal protocol. The five things below will really help you work with international visitors:

1. Try Out A New Skill: Politeness

Business etiquette varies from country to country. As an overall strategy, when greeting and engaging international visitors, be polite and sensitive to how they conduct themselves. For example: If they bow, you can make a slight bow. Don't mimic the depth or duration of their bow because those factors communicate a lot more than you think. If you guess about how far to bow down or how long the bow should be, you could unknowingly barter away your entire sheep herd! Also, match the way they make eye-contact. Don't make direct, lengthy eye contact before you understand what that means to them.

2. Don't Stand So Close To Me

Proxemics is the study of personal space. Otology is the study of ears. Otological Proxemics is the study of the space between your ears. Different cultures have different norms for personal space. In the U.S., when you're having a one-on-one conversation, the personal space is usually between 18 and 30 inches. This could vary in other cultures, so be tuned in to how far visitors stand from you. If they stand way too close, excuse yourself to work up a smelly sweat by sprinting the perimeter of the exhibit hall with only a stop for a garlic and onion slice of pizza. That will make them keep their distance!

3. Put Bold On Hold

Many foreign business people like to build strong personal relationships before launching into the specifics of doing business. I realize cultivating a strong, stable relationship is a real challenge for you, considering you're on your sixth marriage. But don't bring up business issues until you've had plenty of time to schmooze and time for a few introductions. (see next item below)

4. Why Don't We Do It In The Booth

I do it in the exhibit booth all the time. In fact, I recommend you do it in the booth whenever possible. Why? Because foreign visitors really like to meet your executives. Most international business protocol calls for introducing the highest ranking executive first. Also, when exchanging business cards, hold theirs with both hands and actually read it. Then turn it over and check out the back...sometimes there are some internet addresses to great web sites.

5. Leave Your Colloquialisms At Home

Here's a quick list of some basic communication strategies when working with international visitors (thanks to Geoff Alexander):

Avoid metaphors:
  "I've been busy as a one-legged man in a butt-kicking contest!"

Avoid sports analogies:
    "It's fourth and goal at the one, let's go for the TD!"

Avoid slang:
    "Wanna surf the net over a couple of brewskies?"

Avoid regional expressions:
  "I gotta go pawk da caw!" or "I'll have a grinder with that frappe."

INTERNATIONAL VISITOR WORKSHEET

Fill in or checkmark all that apply.

Name:	Company:
Phonetic Spelling:	Address:
Title:	Country:

BODY TYPE/SIZE	CLOTHING
❑ Can easily dunk	❑ Bright, pastel sportcoat
❑ Large human being	❑ Suit and tennis shoes
❑ Short, stout	❑ Jeans and T-shirt
❑ Munchkin	❑ Checks with plaids

HEAD COVERING	NOSE FEATURES
❑ Turban	❑ Long and pointed
❑ Yarmulke	❑ Flat and large
❑ Feathers	❑ Broken
❑ Baseball cap	❑ Runny

EYES	ENGLISH SPEAKING ABILITY
❑ Two	❑ Like a native
❑ Behind Sunglasses	❑ Like a New Yorker
❑ Bloodshot	❑ Challenge to understand
❑ Jaundice	❑ Lots of head nodding

INTERNATIONAL VISITOR QUIZ

Mark whether each statement
is true always, sometimes or never.

STATEMENT	ALWAYS	SOMETIMES	NEVER
1. International visitors talk funny.			
2. I should bow when bowed upon.			
3. Men from Belgium wear lime green sportcoats.			
4. Italians wear charms to ward off evil spirits.			
5. I can tell a foreigner just by looking at him/her.			
6. Foreigners are usually from the Midwest.			

In the first edition,
this page
was left blank.

KEY POINTS

Offending International Visitors

📑 *Be sensitive.*
    Don't dominate with "your" business etiquette.

📑 *Personal space varies.*
    Be aware of how far they stand from you.

📑 *Take time to build relationships.*
    Initially, some international visitors are more
    interested in relationships than in business.

📑 *Colloquialisms = Misunderstandings.*
    Avoid metaphors, sports analogies, slang,
    and regional expressions.

Working With Theater Presentations

It never ceases to amaze me that visitors could be attracted to a large, sweaty man in a spider costume. Maybe it's just me. But you know what, he *was* attracting visitors.

Exhibit booth theaters do attract visitors, some are even qualified, some are not, but everyone should get your message. Why do visitors attend trade show theater presentations? There are 3 reasons: to rest their feet, to get giveaways, and to hear your message. But, that's okay, a full theater is not a bad thing to have, or for visitors to see.

The way I figure it, if the clowns in marketing are going to throw tens of thousands of dollars at theater presentations, take advantage of it. The theater presentation can become a giant qualifying funnel where all visitors are put in at the top and the qualified visitors come out the bottom. For this to happen, the presenter should ask some qualifying questions and ask for a show of hands so visitors can indicate their specific problems time frame for implementing solutions, how long they've been on prozac, etc.

A presenter could say, "Okay, who's looking to buy a new tractor this season?" or "How many of you are ready now to commit to solving your company's hygiene problem?" You should notice who are raising their hands and how often. Those are the visitors you want to speak with after the presentation. When the presentation is over walk up to one of the visitors who was raising his hand and ask, "I noticed a big underarm stain on your shirt when you raised your hand, are you nervous or something." Yes, yes, I know: Icebreakers have been a gift. Finally, the presenter should invite all of the visitors to stay in the booth and visit with the staff. The presenter could even introduce specific staff members, their areas of expertise, and whether they're convicted felons, or just common thugs.

Remember, if 10-20% of the theater attendees stay in the booth to talk to your staff, that's pretty good.

"WHAT ARE THEY THINKING?" QUIZ

Directions: Draw lines to match each person with what they might be thinking during a theater presentation.

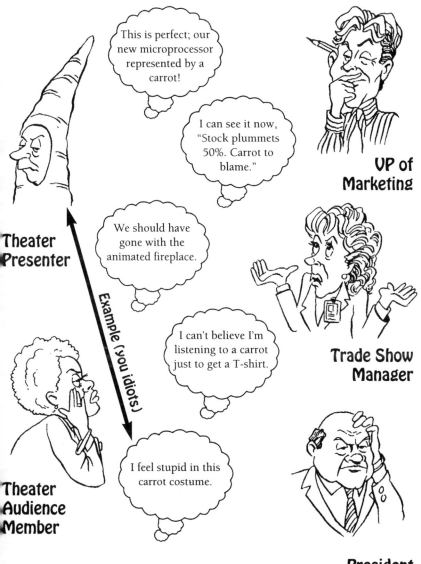

Try not to
think of
a blank page.

KEY POINTS

Working with Theater Presentations

 Take advantage of the gathered audience.

Build qualifying questions into the presentation.

Be proactive about talking with those visitors who, by a show of hands or by head nodding, indicate that they are qualified.

Have the presenter introduce staff responsible for follow-on or more in-depth demonstrations.

Handling Difficult Questions

It's as inevitable as the sun coming up, your CFO embezzling company funds, your sales manager drinking too much or how much you now completely regret throwing your money away on this book. The one or two questions you hope nobody asks invariably get asked and you're going to look like a fool. But hey, you're probably used to that. How can you handle these questions? First, be prepared by anticipating what questions will be asked. Brainstorm some answers. Treat these questions as opportunities to gather more information. Do this by answering their question with your question.

Difficult Question	What You'd Like To Say	What You Can Say
Why are your prices so high?	So we can afford to waste time with visitors like you.	I think we deliver high value products and services. What exactly are you looking for?
When are you going to ship version 3.0 that you announced 3 months ago?	When are you going to stop whining?	Hopefully this quarter. But tell me what you're going to be able to do with 3.0?
What do you think your company's earnings are going to be this quarter?	We're awash in so much red ink that I'm willing to pay you $20 to circulate my résumé at this show.	I'm sorry, but I'm not qualified to answer that. You can call investor relations for an answer.
How do your products compare with those from your competition?	Our competitor's products are junk. In fact, I see them up for sale at garage sales all of the time. You'd be a fool to buy anything from them.	We stack up real well to our competition. Tell me, what is it about their products that you like?
Your product doesn't work the way the brochure said it would.	Lo siento, pero no hablo inglés.	I'm sure we can help. Let's go over and talk to our tech support guy, Bob. Or I can take your card and make certain that someone calls you back.
Hey, how can I get a T-shirt?	Buy something. Actually, I don't think we have size XXXXXXXL to fit you.	Sit through our presentation—we have a drawing and give out one per show.

KEY POINTS

Handling Difficult Questions

Be prepared.
Anticipate tough questions.

Prepare and rehearse answers.

Assemble a list of FAQs (frequently asked questions).

Take control of the conversation.
Answer the question with a question.

Find out why they asked the question.

Treat tough questions as opportunities.
Uncover more information.

Discover more uses for your products/services.

Position yourself as a problem solver.

Group Dynamics

A New Concept: Be Productive

The biggest increases in productivity you will ever make in the exhibit booth will result from either:

1. Effectively managing groups of visitors, or

2. Somehow acquiring a new personality.

Imagine how much more productive you would be if you asked a group assembled around you, "Everyone who is planning to buy within the next 30 days, has the budget to buy, and has influence on the decision to buy, please stay for a few more minutes. I'd like to thank the rest of you for stopping by, have a great show."

This is called group qualifying and dismissing. Imagine how well this would work on your in-laws.

Verbal, Nonverbal, and Herbal Techniques

Engage and include visitors who walk up in the middle of a conversation or demonstration by first making eye contact and then stepping to the side. This nonverbally invites them to join by opening up a space for them. This one small step for a (wo)man and one giant leap for productivity will communicate your intentions to both the visitor you began with and the one(s) wishing to join the group.

Next:

(1) verbally greet them (say something, you idiot!)

(2) summarize the conversation—this will really make them feel like part of the group; and

(3) ask them if this topic is of interest to them. If they're merely scrounging for recyclable trash (behavior usually associated with regional sales managers), try to cut a deal for a percentage of the redemption value.

As the group grows, begin speaking to the entire group *as a group.* Have them do things as a group; like jeering your competitors or mocking your least favorite company executive.

Do the Group Grope

Now you should have the situation set up for real productivity; group qualifying, dismissing, and closing. When you can move from working with one or two visitors to engaging, including, and directing a continually growing group of visitors, you will be a true exhibit pro.

The group dynamics skills you will need to do this consistently are very challenging to learn and master. This is probably too much to ask of anyone, especially of you. Your potential for developing and mastering these skills would probably dictate you being permanently assigned the job of booth brochure monitor.

Interrupt Me, Please
Your usual rude behavior is okay in the booth.

There are no private conversations in the public areas of the booth. That means two things: 1. Anyone can be interrupted at any time, and 2. If you want a private conversation, make it happen in a conference room or outside the booth.

Let's see how this works using a real-life scenario: You've discovered that the visitor you're talking to needs to talk to your company's chicken plucking expert, Bob. But Bob is talking with his own visitor. Normally, you and the visitor would end up waiting for Bob. Instead, politely interrupt Bob when he's talking, not when the visitor's talking, and inform him that a visitor is waiting to talk with him. Then ask him how long he'll be. Bob can say, "Oh just a couple of minutes." This communicates two things. First, that Bob's visitor only has a

couple of minutes left and second, that the visitor you brought
over only has to wait a couple of minutes. Or Bob can say,
"Actually, if it's okay with you (he asks his visitor) you can join
in on our conversation right now."

Wrong Way to Interrupt

Better Way to Interrupt

GROUP DYNAMICS QUIZ

Which groups are most likely to visit your booth?

1.

2.

3.

4.

KEY POINTS

Group Dynamics

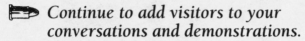 *Continue to add visitors to your conversations and demonstrations.*

    Make eye contact.

    Greet them.

    Take a step back or to the side to non-verbally invite them to join your group.

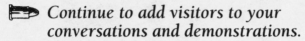 *Group control skills.*

    Be in control.

    Get the group to do something; fill out lead forms, visit other stations or areas in the exhibit booth, etc.

    Qualify and dismiss people en mass; as a group, to be most productive.

© The Hill Group • (408) 257-7828

CROWD CONTROL

Move along lil' doggies

It's a fluke; your booth is really busy. Maybe it's even like your nose...congested and noisy. What could explain this?

1. Could it be because of the compelling message your booth is communicating with its neon outline of Michael Jackson?

2. Perhaps it's the exciting new products all the visitors want to see...your new non-mechanical pencil and the electronic coffee cup?

3. Wait, maybe it's busy because of the trained, professional looking staff...you wish!

4. There is always, of course, that slight chance that everyone is attracted by your giveaway...no, in this case probably not...who wants Beatle Reunion Concert tickets anyway?

The Question of Congestion

Is a congested booth good? There are pros and cons. Pros: (1) Gives the appearance that something exciting is going on or there is something interesting to see, (2) Great opportunity to maximize leads, (3) Great opportunity to communicate your message to a lot of people at the same time, and (4) Great opportunity to pick-pocket rich-looking visitors.

Cons: (1) Some visitors will postpone, or avoid, a visit to a congested booth, (2) Visitor satisfaction is in jeopardy (they're used to getting one-on-one attention), (3) You might miss some opportunities to meet with hot prospects, and (4) It's a lot of noise when you're hungover.

Few companies take advantage of the real opportunity at trade shows—making congestion and crowds work for them. With proper implementation of my crowd control skills and techniques, you'll want congestion. So grab your cattle prod!

Working With ~~Sheep~~ Visitors

When your booth is congested, it requires crowd control. Here are some handy tips:

1. Visitors will usually do what you ask of them, so ask them to do what you want.

2. They will usually follow you anywhere; start walking and they will too.

3. They are usually cooperative; especially if given a reasonable rationale or explanation.

4. Get them moving by giving them something to do; "Here, take this lead form over there and fill it out."

5. Crowds beget crowds (that means a crowd of people attracts more people). Be ready to make smaller groups out of larger ones so no one can escape some personal attention.

6. Get them moving or doing by giving them a SMART objective. "Go see Cecilee over there right now and ask her about multitasking multimedia multiplexers."

7. Visitors will often make unsecured personal loans. Try this reasonable request at your next show: "Excuse me sir, could I borrow $55 for lunch?"

CROWD CONTROL ESSAY QUESTIONS

1. Briefly describe why people act like, and sometimes smell like, sheep.

2. Describe a situation at the last show you worked where a crowd turned on you because you're an obnoxious, arrogant human being.

3. Why don't most companies use crowd control psychology when asking for volunteers to explain to the CEO why your company's name is misspelled?

4. What is the relationship between the distance from floor to pant cuffs on visitors to their tendency to do whatever you tell them?

If this page
were blank,
I'd say so
in writing.

KEY POINTS

Crowd Control

Ask crowds of visitors to do things:

To follow you.

To fill out lead forms.

To listen to your presentation.

Crowds will follow you if you take action:

If you want them to follow you, start walking.

Give them something to hold and/or something to do.

Direct them to a specific station and person.

If what you want a visitor or crowd to do is reasonable, give them the rationale.

© The Hill Group • (408) 257-7828

THE BASICS

What You Should Already Know

Working a trade show is probably the most difficult selling job there is, except of course for convincing your manager that you do have viable sales prospects in Maui.

Trade shows are a combination of retail sales, outside sales, marketing, entertainment, and just plain hard work. But it's show time on the exhibit floor when those doors open and the ~~diots~~ visitors pour in. Lights! Camera! $8 hot dogs! Action!

When you're "on stage," defined as anytime you can be identified with your company, you've got to be on your best behavior. If you're wearing that company name tag, you represent your entire company no matter where you are; in line for a Vodka Collins before breakfast, in the bathroom, or even on the Sheriff's bus for your arraignment on felony "useless human being" charges.

Visitors Don't Like You

Remember the basics. Don't give any visitor any reason not to talk with you. The priority is to influence sales by having meaningful interactions with as many visitors as possible, sort of the opposite of what is happening in your family life.

If you're talking with your colleagues, talking on the phone, eating, drinking, or have your back to aisle working with a computer, most visitors will wait...or they won't wait...until you're finished. The basics of professional booth behavior will ensure that you're approachable and likeable. Don't worry, I'm sure these "nice person" traits are only temporary.

This story illustrates my point. I was at a show last February. When I got to my client's booth, I noticed they had a little machine that would take a business card and make it into a luggage tag. It's incredible! This new technology just blows me away! Anyway, I'm so excited that I immediately get some venture capital and open four mall stores, all next to Macy's. Six months later, here I am trying to get you to pop for this book.

THE BASICS

Smile! We just got this picture of one of your colleagues during a trade show.

Can you name 7 things that are wrong with this picture?

Answers are upside down below.

4. *No eating in the booth*

7. *No dynamite in the booth*   3. *No drinking in the booth*

6. *No idiots in the booth*   2. *No TV watching in the booth*

5. *No smoking in the booth*   1. *No sitting in the booth*

You win.
Go ahead
and read
this blank page.

Key Points

The Basics

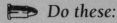 *Do these:*

Smile.

Be enthusiastic.

Be motivated to meet the objectives.

Treat visitors as guests.

Be professional.

Keep the booth neat and clean.

Demonstrate open, receptive body language.

© The Hill Group • (408) 257-7828

KEY POINTS CONTINUED

The Basics

 Don't do these:

Eat in the booth.

Drink in the booth.

Talk too much among yourselves.

Read in the booth.

Use the phone in the booth.

Leave the booth or your station unattended.

BONUS SECTION: HOW TO BE ARROGANT.
Just act like:

1. Your customers
- ✔ Wander around aimlessly.
- ✔ Expect your own company to serve you.
- ✔ Know little or nothing about your exhibit booth.

2. An outside salesperson
- ✔ Work only with your own customers.
- ✔ Talk with only the people you want to for as long as you want to.
- ✔ Ignore visitors and talk with other salespeople.

3. A jerk
- ✔ Show up late.
- ✔ Don't attend any pre-show meetings.
- ✔ Leave the booth without telling anyone.

4. An important employee
- ✔ Act like you have better things to do than talk to visitors.
- ✔ Don't help keep the booth neat and clean. It's probably somebody else's responsibility.
- ✔ Schmooze only with people who can help you.

SON OF BONUS SECTION:
HOW TO BE A TRADE SHOW ~~IDIAT~~ IDIOT.

Treat the exhibit booth like:

1. A restaurant
- ✔ Eat in the booth, especially popcorn.
- ✔ Drink in the booth, with a straw, making loud slurping noises.
- ✔ Expect your own people to serve you. Pull rank.

2. Your living room
- ✔ Sit on chairs, counters, couches; hey, your feet hurt.
- ✔ Talk loudly about non-work subjects; sports & gossip.
- ✔ Ignore people that walk up; you do it at home.

3. A party
- ✔ Stand around in circles and talk to your colleagues.
- ✔ Don't forget to put both hands in your pockets.

4. A bar
- ✔ Use the exhibit booth as a pick-up place.
- ✔ Engage in loud conversation and laughing.
- ✔ Down a couple of drinks at lunch.

5. A place to be hungover
- ✔ Drink heavily and stay out late in the evenings.
- ✔ Don't brush your teeth.

The Hill Group takes a fresh approach to training your exhibit staff. We believe your people should have fun working in the exhibit booth and they should stay focused on the show objectives.

I'm fed up with you.
This page is blank.
Quit reading it or
I'm calling the police.